HOW TO APOLOGIZE

David LaRochelle   illustrated by Mike Wohnoutka

CANDLEWICK PRESS

Everyone makes mistakes.

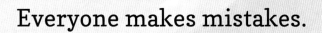

Whether you are big . . .

or small.

And when you've made a mistake that has hurt someone or something, the right thing to do is apologize.

Apologizing can be hard, especially
if the other person is mad . . .

or if it's someone you don't like.

But it's important to apologize anyway—even if that person owes you an apology too.

Your apology can be simple:
Tell the other person you're sorry for what you did.

Don't make excuses.

NO

I'm usually much more careful but I had an itch on my knee and a mosquito flew down my throat and I was trying to avoid a dangerous-looking crack in the sidewalk and if your ladder wasn't taking up so much space I wouldn't have bumped into it.

And be sincere.

NOT SINCERE

Mom told me I had to apologize for putting your doll in the fishbowl or I can't go outside and play baseball. So I'm sorry.

NOT SINCERE

Ha! Ha! I'm sorry I "accidentally" squirted you with the garden hose when you were weeding the flower bed. Hee! Hee! But you have to admit you look hilarious. Ha! Ha! Ha!

NOT SINCERE

Look at the new GLOW-IN-THE-DARK WATCH I got for my birthday and I'm having a CUPCAKE PARTY on Saturday and I'm sorry I sat on your violin and guess who's going to be the STAR of the DANCE RECITAL next week . . . ME!

SINCERE

I'm sorry I popped your balloon. I really am.

You can also apologize with a note.

Even if the mistake happened a long time ago,

Do you remember back in 1987 when I called you pokey-pants?

Yes.

it's never too late to apologize.

I'm sorry.

Thank you.

If possible, try to fix the mistake.

But sometimes you can't.

In that case, you can still say you're sorry, then take steps to avoid making the same mistake again.

We're very, very sorry!

It might be difficult, but apologizing will make you feel better.

More importantly, it will make the other person feel better.

And that's why we apologize.

For Dennis Christian, who taught me how to apologize
DL

To my friend David LaRochelle
MW

Text copyright © 2021 by David LaRochelle
Illustrations copyright © 2021 by Mike Wohnoutka

First edition 2021

Library of Congress Catalog Card Number 2021934571
ISBN 978-1-5362-0944-0

22 23 24 25 26 TLF 10 9 8 7 6

Printed in Dongguan, Guangdong, China

This book was typeset in Copse.
The illustrations were done in gouache.

Candlewick Press
99 Dover Street
Somerville, Massachusetts 02144

www.candlewick.com

Oops! I'm sorry!